Frien
Friendship to R
Attraction, Become Desirable, Get The Girl

By Patrick King
Dating and Social Skills Coach at
www.PatrickKingConsulting.com

Table of Contents

Introduction

When I was a sophomore in high school, I thought I had it all figured out.

I was in calculus a year early, was the starting right midfielder for the soccer team, and I recently got the ***best friend label*** from the girl that I so coveted, Sharon. That was the first step winning her over as my **girlfriend**, right?

Honestly, I thought I had it in the bag. We had been friends ever since the day we met in the third grade. We sat next to each other during "duck, duck, goose" and instantly hit it off over the topic of Lunchables and how amazing they were. (I maintain that stance to this day)

In hindsight, it was clear that I always had a **crush** on her. I treated her so differently from the rest of my 'normal' friends, and gave her a ton of special attention. I bent over backwards for her, and generally catered to her every whim. **Some might call this one-itis.**

Whether consciously or subconsciously, I thought that she operated on some kind of **affection meter**. Once her meter was filled up from my acts of service and gestures, I imagined that two things would happen. First, she would begin to realize how much I meant to her, and second, she would realize how much she depended on me in her life... *and suddenly sexual and romantic attraction would follow.*

Welcome to what I've termed the **platonic backdoor gambit**. Hint – it almost *never* works, for two main reasons.

First, it depends on the female being a mind-reader. I never asked her out and just depended on her to figure out what I wanted and take action **for** me.

Second, it assumes that treating a woman like a best friend and becoming emotionally intimate with her keeps you firmly **out** of the Friendzone. Counterintuitively, it cements your status there if you don't pair that with what women find instinctually attractive.

I got a firsthand look at that when one of my **soccer teammates** who barely knew Sharon started showing interest and flirting with her in class and after school.

I thought that he had no chance compared to me because I was so emotionally in tuned with her, and knew exactly how to take care of her... or so I thought.

He teased her, was playful with her, and generally wasn't attentive to her in the ways that I was. He mostly said whatever he wanted and wasn't always concerned with how he was perceived by her. The **biggest shock** to me was that I noticed that he would act the same way with most females, and this actually seemed to make them like him more.

All the while, Sharon would tell me that I was such a *good friend* for listening to her talk about my teammate. It seemed that my platonic backdoor gambit was not paying dividends.

Where did I go wrong? It was pretty simple, actually.

When you present yourself as a **friend**, women essentially have no choice but to put you in the Friendzone, even if they were initially interested. This is doubly true when you present yourself as a friend, but don't treat her like a normal female friend with the platonic backdoor gambit.

But when you present yourself as a **potential mate** by making your intentions clear, flirting, and using the power of physical touch, you force women to treat you as such and make an **actual choice** about how to view you. The important part is that you even give yourself a chance, and that you aren't automatically placed into the Friendzone.

That simple mindset shift is what my soccer teammate embodied. And yes, it can be scary as hell when you feel that you will potentially sacrifice your friendship with someone if things don't work out.

But if you've had intentions towards her the entire time, **I've got news for you**. You didn't really have the friendship you thought you did, and you don't really know her like you thought you did.

Naturally, this can put some men at a loss. How do you reset years of conditioning about what you thought women wanted, and start presenting yourself as a potential mate? What's the real difference?

Friendzone Proof has all those answers. You'll read about how you can tell where on the spectrum you fall, and exactly what you can do about it. You can reset expectations with just a different approach. **This book is going to change the way you interact with females.**

It's a journey that I'm intimately familiar with, for better or worse. The **pain**, the feelings of **neglect**, and the leaps of faith are all things that seemed like a dark tunnel until I saw the light at the end of the road.

The girl you've always wanted? There's no reason you can't get her – except **you**.

1. A tale of two ladders.

In a relationship that is ambiguously platonic between men and women, one of the worst places a man can ever find himself is the **Friendzone**.

If you are interested in being more than a friend to that special female friend in your life, the Friendzone is your **graveyard**, your **Waterloo**. You would be better off just now knowing her than being stuck in the Friendzone.

In the Friendzone, that woman treats you as she would a girlfriend or **gay** male friend.

Neither situation is ideal, though in the beginning you might think it is progress in the right direction. You would like to be her lover, so isn't building a strong **foundation of friendship** the best way to get to that point?

Yes and no. At the end of the day you are still just her friend, a foundation that may or may not grow the way you want it to.

Does this mean that there is no **intimacy** between you two? Absolutely not. In fact, the Friendzone can be one of the most intimate places you will ever inhabit. And this is precisely what makes it so **frustrating and counterintuitive** to men.

You get all the **emotional** intimacy but none of the **physical** intimacy. Just as you might have really close friends with whom you share everything, that special female will share everything with you except one thing – **her body**. This is exactly how a woman treats her female friends.

Understandably, many guys want to get the hell out of the Friendzone as quickly as possible.

The prevailing conception of the Friendzone involves the notion of **two ladders** – a context that I find easy to explain. This theory says that there are only two ways into the life of a special female - the **friend** ladder (Friendzone), and the **relationship** ladder.

Let me preface this by saying that while I enjoy the framework of the ladder theory, I don't think it necessarily holds up … indeed, if you find yourself on the wrong ladder, **this very book** will show you how to leap to the ladder you want.

The ladder theory.

According to this theory, men start off as **neutral** parties with females.

But soon there are **two invisible ladders** in front of you with regards to how that female starts looking at you - the friend ladder, and the relationship ladder. You need to choose very carefully how you act around a female early on because she will very quickly designate you to one of the two ladders.

Once you have gone up that friendship ladder, that special female has labeled you her friend and permanently cast you in that role. There is no hope of being reclassified as someone other than a friend. You are trapped forever in a platonic relationship with her.

You are stuck on the top rung of the ladder with no way down, and absolutely no way to get to the other ladder. You simply can't make the leap across that chasm.

Therefore, **early on** you must act in a way that puts you onto the relationship ladder. If you want to be in a relationship with that woman, and if you want sex to be part of the relationship, you have to act like it from the outset.

This ladder theory is very simple, and this is precisely why it is so popular with men. You only need to focus on one or the other. It is a straightforward and easy game plan. Everything is viewed in black and white and it's an all or nothing proposition. **Simple**, yes?

Of course not. Life is anything but black and white. We may aspire to the black and white, the cut and dry, the absolute, but in truth we spend 99% of our time in **shades of gray**.

The ladder theory is **absolutely wrong**. It doesn't match reality.

The reality is that you can start off as friends, and become lovers later on. And, it works the **opposite** way: many relationships often progress from sexual relationships to great deep and lasting permanent life-long friendships.

Starting off on one ladder doesn't mean you can't jump from ladder to ladder. It is no surprise that the ladder theory is wrong; it over-simplifies all the things that can go right and wrong in a relationship with that special woman and it only offers two choices.

Human relationships are very complicated. We have different emotions. We have different ways of looking at things. We have different spins we can put on the many complicated, and often confusing, things that happen in our lives.

It is unfair, in terms of **human potential**, to reduce everything into a black and white choice.

But if you think you are going to end up on the wrong ladder and there is nothing you can do about it, **that's what will happen**. Believing that you can't control your own actions and your own fate becomes a **self-fulfilling prophecy**.

So why do so many guys bemoan the fact that they are on the wrong ladder? Why can't they make that very doable jump? The reasons are what I'm going to talk about in this book.

Men, when they present themselves as friends, **become friends**. They don't overtly show their intentions. They just *hope* to make the woman fall in love with them through **implied** or indirect means. They don't behave like a potential mate. Instead they act like a friend that is vaguely **sycophantic and obsessive**.

And yet, when we think about what women want, it's someone who is assertive and more direct, isn't it? It's the more **direct** guys that get themselves onto the more-than-friends ladder.

Timing is indisputably an important factor as well.

The guys on the relationship ladder know that you have to **strike** while the iron is hot. You have to get close to her, not hesitate or linger too long, then make your move. Guys who find themselves in the Friendzone are guys who get really close to a girl, then fail to make a move. They are so afraid of being rejected they **freeze** up. This **analysis paralysis** makes them exactly the kind of guy that women aren't attracted to.

You have to make sure that your intentions are understood. You have to make it clear that you don't want to be in the Friendzone, that you want something **more**.

You have to get over your fear. Focus on what you will **gain** instead of what you are afraid of losing. This is the key to avoiding the Friendzone.

Okay, so the ladder theory is wrong, but it doesn't mean it's that easy to get out of the Friendzone. **In theory** it is simple, but many men cannot find their way to the correct ladder because the habits and behaviors they exhibit around women they desire are so deeply ingrained.

It's a cycle - once you are **typecast** as a friend, it is very hard to establish a new role as a lover so you continue acting like a friend. You move up a few rungs on *that* ladder making it even harder to reset the relationship and jump ladders. You get so accustomed to acting in a certain way (a *friend* way) that you forget how to **actually pursue** a woman. Instead, you're trying to get high enough on the friend ladder that it snaps and gives you a **bridge** to the relationship ladder. Good luck with that.

It's an epidemic borne out of lack of awareness and fear of rejection. Men often aren't aware that they are on the wrong ladder until it's too late. They lose sight of what women are attracted to. Then, they are so comfortable and content with the friend-relationship they have cultivated with the woman that they fail to take action and are **afraid** to **jiggle the ladder** they are standing on. Sound familiar?

2. What causes the Friendzone?

Here's one of the worst parts about the Friendzone – you are usually the **last** person to find out that you are in it.

You were attracted to that woman the first time you met her. You always wanted to be more than friends with her. This all started on day one.

The problem is that you got really close to her and **didn't make a move**. You focused on building an emotional connection first.

Sometimes there is actually some **sexual tension**. In the past, there might have been lots of opportunities for you to go beyond just being a friend. The problem is, the more **opportunities** you let slip through your fingers, the more **concrete** it is becomes in the woman's mind that you just want to be friends.

She's usually **following your lead** because that's what women do in potential relationships... and when you fail to capitalize on the sexual tension that might have existed in the beginning, (1) it fades, (2) she gets bored and loses interest, or (3) she decides that you really only want to be friends. Often it's a combination of all three.

Why does she move on so quickly? We men simply have no concept of how overwhelming it can be for women to have so many options available to them.

So you can see why, from a practical perspective, it makes complete sense that women feel they need to put people into **distinct zones**. It's just housekeeping for the parts of their brains that dictate romantic attraction and chemistry. Either you're interested and it's a potential relationship, or you're not interested and she won't waste her time thinking of you that way.

It is easy to put all the blame on the woman and say, "*Well, she just automatically throws guys in there*." But in most cases, the blame lays squarely on the guys' shoulders. They were just too slow on the draw and **forced** the woman to categorize him that way.

You have to get off the fence very quickly. Once you decide that this woman is worth chasing, you have actually do it. You have to decide that this woman is worth the risk of looking like a fool – and then you have to actually **take that risk**.

If you don't want to end up in the Friendzone, you must understand why the Friendzone happens. Learn to recognize **patterns** in your relationships that land you in that zone so that you can make the necessary adjustments.

<u>Women don't like confrontation.</u>

Many guys like to play nice and sweet, and they hope that the girls will notice their **passive** efforts. They hope that just by playing nice, women will be bowled over by their niceness and figure out for themselves how attractive they are.

The guys think that by being super nice, women will be so impressed they will automatically reclassify them as **relationship material**.

What is wrong with this picture?

If you are going to play nice and hope that women will notice your passive efforts, you are playing a **losing game**. Nothing comes from passive efforts except a feeling of resentment and bitterness when the expected reward inevitably does not materialize.

You cannot play the dating game in a passive manner and hope that things will swing your way. That's like expecting women to present themselves to you on your doorstep, simply because you followed the **linear steps** one, two, and three.

If you are interested in a woman, **be direct**. Make it clear to her that you want to be something more than friends.

If you don't do this, guess what?

Women are far more anti-confrontational than men, so they'll never tell you that your efforts at winning their affections are **doomed to fail**. They will just silently drop you in the Friendzone and hope everything sorts itself out –

in other words, that you get the **hint** and leave her alone.

You didn't strike while the iron was hot. You didn't make your move. You let opportunities slip by you. The more sexual and intimate opportunities you let pass, the harder it will be to get out of the Friendzone. Why? Her view of you as "just a friend" will become stronger and more fixed.

Eventually, it will reach a point where she will be shocked to find out that you were sexually attracted to her.

By playing things passively and allowing women to avoid confrontation, you have allowed your relationship to become strictly platonic.

The platonic backdoor gambit.

You have probably seen this in high school. Guys try to be **best friends** with women they want. It's a **label** that they practically beg for and revel in.

They'll bend over backwards for a woman, but in the name of an altruistic and giving friendship – **not** in any romantic capacity. They try to fly **under the radar** and build a platonic connection that is so strong it will **morph** into a romantic attraction. All the while, the woman is clearly not interested and is simply enjoying being treated well and having attention heaped on her.

The problem is that you didn't really want her to be your friend. You wanted something else and had an **ulterior motive**. You end up chasing after something that isn't really there because you have deluded yourself into it.

The platonic backdoor gambit is based on a **faulty** premise: the premise that you can turn **mud into marble**.

If you want to be in a relationship with a woman, you have to pick women who are, at the very least, *somewhat* interested in having you as a lover. Otherwise, you are going to have a tough time trying to convert a woman who is absolutely not interested in you as a lover into one by first turning her into a friend.

I'm not saying that the platonic backdoor gambit doesn't work at all. It has a low chance of succeeding so it would be unwise to completely dismiss it. It *does* happen that a guy and a girl start off as reluctant friends and become lovers later on.

But realize that is the **exception to the rule**; it is not a smart way to create the attraction you want and need to be Friendzone proof.

3. Signs to recognize the Friendzone.

I mentioned before that **lack of awareness** is a large contributor to ending up in the Friendzone.

Just like flies that find themselves caught in a spider web, guys who find themselves in the Friendzone got there because they weren't **paying attention**.

They were minding their own business, thinking that they were making good progress with this woman by getting her to open up emotionally.

If you don't mind getting treated like a girlfriend, then the Friendzone can be a fine place. If you don't mind not having sex with the woman you are interested in, the Friendzone can be quite pleasant.

It is like the **Bermuda triangle** of romantic relationships. A lot of guys go in, but very few come out.

The first step in avoiding any kind of situation is learning how to recognize it. Recognize what preceding steps lead to the particular set of circumstances that you want to avoid. Simple **pattern** recognition that, when brought to light, can save time and a whole lot of heartache.

She calls you her friend.

If she keeps mentioning the word "friend" a lot, that is a sign. She's using that word very **carefully**, and using it very prominently in front of you in the hope that you will pick up on the **hint**.

She sees you **only** as a friend, and wants to deliver that message to you.

Does this mean that sex is out of the picture? Does this mean that a potential romantic relationship is completely impossible? Absolutely not. But the deck is stacked against you. She is looking at you primarily as a friend for now, and wants you to be aware of that she is not interested in more.

This means you have to send the right signals so she can stop viewing you as a platonic friend and start building an attraction. Don't put her on a pedestal. Make your intentions known, but don't bend over backwards for her.

This is very important because we label things in the world based on how we mentally construct the world. If you let her **verbal labels** of you slip by unnoticed or unaddressed, you have a first class ticket to the Friendzone.

Calling you her gay best friend or her brother.

If she tries to pass you off to her friends as her gay best friend or her brother, this is a **red flag**. There is nothing derogatory about calling you her gay best friend. What she is saying is that she has a deep and profound trust in you, that she feels completely safe around you.

A lot of guys completely misread this and think it is a great **compliment**. While you should not be insulted when a female calls you a gay best friend, you should be alarmed at this label because of what it indicates regarding your romantic prospects.

This isn't an issue if you just want her as a friend. If you just want to hang around her, or treat her like a little sister, this designation is not a big deal. It is a big deal, however, if you want more than a pseudo-sibling relationship.

Again, just like being called a friend, being treated like a brother or a gay best friend doesn't necessarily mean there is no hope with that person. But you have to **counteract** these signals because they indicate how she feels about you – not as a heterosexual male that is available to date.

No immediate sexual attraction or tension.

If you can't feel immediate sexual attraction from her, or there is no sexual tension when you are around each other, you should **break away** very quickly. Unfortunately, many guys find this hard to do. They think that just being within **five feet** of this woman is a victory.

This is absolutely wrong. Winning has been incorrectly defined and sometimes includes some incredibly low standards for Friendzoned men.

You are shooting yourself in the foot if you continue to hang out with her when you don't really feel that she is sexually attracted to you. If you don't feel any type **of sexual tension**, it means that the physical signals you are sending her way are not registering properly. This is controllable by **you** for the most part, and it means that you haven't acted in a way that creates sexual attraction or tension.

This also means that the pattern you are establishing by hanging out and basically considering yourself lucky just to be around her is sending her the **wrong signals**. You are making her comfortable around you as a friend.

If you want her to be romantically attracted to you, there has to be some sort of tension. There has to be some sort of **sexual discomfort** that builds up over time and can only be **resolved** by something more intimate and physical. This is not the case when you keep hanging around her like a puppy dog and feel lucky to have that **privilege**. Tension is built through challenge and intrigue, and a puppy dog nipping at your heels, desperate for your attention, embodies the opposite.

So if you haven't built the tension with the correct approach on your first pass, you should **disengage** and approach her later in a better way.

That way, the right kind of sexual attraction and tension will exist and make you Friendzone proof.

Make sure that you never get on the friendship ladder at all.

The real problem with the ladder theory is that it is a self-fulfilling prophecy. Many guys would rather have that special girl in their life as a friend than risk not having her in their life at all because they took a chance on love.

I'm sorry to say this to you, but if that is your attitude, you deserve to be in the Friendzone. It is much better to be on the **lowest rung** of the relationship ladder, regardless of how fumbling and futile it may seem at first, than spend all kinds of time and emotional effort on the friendship ladder where the result of your efforts only lands you where you don't want to be.

Regardless of the signals you are getting, if you suspect somehow that you are in the Friendzone, **walk away**. Never be afraid of walking away from that special woman. Regardless of how she looks, or how she makes you feel, or how awesome you think your future romantic or sexual relationship with her would be, walk away and reset your chances.

The fact that you are **unhappy** that you aren't with her and are pining for her means that you really would be happier taking a chance on love. It's scary, I get it. But the **cost-benefit ratio** is strongly in favor of taking a chance instead of always wondering "what if" and wasting your life.

4. Pedestals and the Friendzone.

The funny thing about the Friendzone is that the more you try to avoid it, the more it gets to you. It is like sinking into **quicksand**. The more you struggle, the faster you sink.

People who successfully get out of quicksand are people who remain calm. They play it cool. They don't freak out.

The Friendzone is emotional quicksand.

Here you are in the Friendzone, bending over backwards for her, treating her like a queen, making her the priority of your life. At the end of the day, she walks out into the sunset and into a bright new tomorrow with a guy who, obviously, doesn't deserve her. She deserves only the best because she is so special. Talk about getting your heart crushed.

One of the best ways to avoid the Friendzone is take off your rose-colored glasses and **not** to make that extra special woman in your life a special priority. You've put her on a pedestal if you believe all of the above, and made her someone that you feel you can never get.

Have you ever noticed that when you ignore a **cat**, it comes up to you and brushes its tail in your face? On the other hand, if you are extra nice to the cat, it turns its nose up at you as it passes by, as if you don't exist.

The same dynamic plays out when it comes to women.

When you put a woman on a pedestal, it signals to her that she is above you, you are not her **equal**, and there will never be a chance for a romantic relationship. Who wants to be with someone who signals that they are inferior to them and is going to cater to their every desire? It sounds attractive and romantic at the beginning, but it will quickly succumb to reality: people are attracted to **challenge**.

People want what they can't have, and take for granted what they have in front of them. It's generic and hackneyed, but extremely applicable to the Friendzone and to putting women up on pedestals. If you give a woman too much and make yourself too **available**, they will be turned off by it and automatically throw you into the friend bucket – it's just not what she's looking for in a **romantic partner**.

If you don't want to be in the Friendzone, treat her no differently than you treat your friends. Don't make her any more of a priority than you would a normal friend.

Don't make her feel that you are putting your life on hold just for her. Don't dump all the other important things in your life just for her. Don't bend over backwards for her, if you wouldn't bend over backwards for your other friends.

When you do this, you are sending out a clear signal to her.

You are saying, "*You are not on a pedestal. I am not going to deny myself living a full life just for you.*"

The problem with the Friendzone is that it is a confusing place where sexual desire and romantic desire are intertwined with love for friends. We all love our friends. That is why they are our friends. But it is a completely platonic kind of love.

Unfortunately, guys in the Friendzone often put that special woman on a pedestal when she is just a friend. She looks at you only as a friend. Her love for you is that of a friend. Unfortunately, she knows she's on that pedestal, and it is completely **flattering**.

What is wrong with this picture? You are like a court jester who will make a fool of himself for her, elevate her, and make *her* feel great. You would cut out your heart so she could feel better about herself. This is all great for her, but at the end of the day, you are still just a friend in her eyes. Guess who's holding the **short end** of that stick?

You don't put your friends on pedestals. Friends are friends because they are real. Friends benefit us so much because we push back against them. We challenge them, and they challenge us. They keep us real.

You make your friends cry sometimes. You make your friends **hurt** sometimes. Why? It is because they do the same to you. That is what makes it a human relationship. That is what keeps that relationship's feet **planted** solidly on the ground.

This is what separates real friendships from fake friendships. Fake friendships don't grow. Fake friendships hit a certain level and **stagnate**.

But if you are looking for real friends - friends who help you explore your soul and make you a better person, friends who help you explore the wide and far boundaries of life - then these are friendships worth crying over. These are friendships worth getting mad over, because you are dealing with real people.

Real people aren't always nice to each other. Real friends aren't always pleasant to each other. This is why you shouldn't put them on a pedestal. You shouldn't rope them off with some sort of emotional velvet cord.

Feel free to ignore them. Feel free to push back. Feel free to be upset.

Most important, you don't bend over backwards for your friends if they don't for you. You just don't. Ultimately, when you are doing this, you are afraid of offending them or of **losing** their friendship.

If you feel that you are bending over backwards for your friends, stop it. You are not being a friend. Either you are real friends and you are typecasting them to become fake friends, or you are setting yourself up to be Friendzoned by that special female whose heart you want to win.

5. Non-confrontation leads to the Friendzone.

Almost all guys who find themselves in the Friendzone share one feature: they never actually flirt with the target of their affections.

They think that all they need to do to make this woman fall in love with them is to be super nice to her. They think that women are mind readers. "*She will know my affections for her, and she will reciprocate.*"

This kind of thinking is magical and not rooted in reality. Just as it would be foolish to live your life based on magical formulas, you have to be more **obvious and direct** regarding your actions with women.

If you want a woman to feel the same attraction for you that you do for her, show or tell her of your attraction. Unfortunately, fear is what drives many guys into the Friendzone. By playing it safe and being Nice Guy, they hide their hand. They try to be sneaky about it because they are afraid of taking direct action.

They know they want a romantic relationship, but they are so afraid of being rejected that they try to use a **backdoor**.

This **Trojan horse** approach usually doesn't work out because you haven't been clear. You have to remember that you are not the only romantic prospect for that special woman you want to be with. You are not the only game in town as far as her emotions and sexual attractions are concerned.

In fact, if you are drawn to a very attractive woman, you can bet so are many **other guys**. And guess what? They will be more **upfront** and transparent regarding their intent.

This is why guys who constantly find themselves in the Friendzone need to wake up. They need to learn how to flirt with the woman they want to go to bed with. Make your **intent** known.

Letting someone know your intentions will open up the possibility of her seeing you as more than a friend. Without your being direct, she may not have any idea of what you want. Once she knows how you feel, she will be able to visualize dating you – and **visualization** is the first step to action. You can't assume she knows where you stand without being direct, and you shouldn't rely on her reading your mind or being able to infer from your actions alone what your intent is.

Don't act like regular friends in **all** ways.

I know this seems to contradict what I mentioned in the previous chapter, but there's a big distinction here.

I said you should treat the object of your affections as you do your other friends. That means don't show her the kind of special treatment that puts her on a pedestal. Here what I am saying is that you should **not** treat her like a friend because you don't flirt and show sexual attraction to your regular female friends.

If you see that there is not much difference between how you act with her and how her other friends act with her, you shouldn't be surprised that you are squarely in the Friendzone. She is treating you like a friend because that is the role you've taken on.

So what's the solution? It's **flirting**, it's **bantering**, and it's creating **chemistry**. Otherwise, you are just another girlfriend to her. At some point, it's also making your intentions towards her known, which is definitely something that her girlfriends don't do.

Don't be afraid to touch her. In this way, you might want to envision treating her more like a girlfriend than a regular friend.

Don't let her be oblivious to your affections.

Don't let her overlook or mischaracterize what you are feeling for her. Women are very smart creatures. They have a label for everything, and they avoid confrontation ... so they might very well know what you are trying to do, but will act **oblivious** for the sake of peace. When she tries to put you on an emotional shelf where you don't belong, be obvious and direct about your affections.

Make it **clear** to the woman you are trying to attract that you are interested in her. You can do this in a joking way, or you can do it in a serious way. What is important is that you need to move the idea from *your* heart into *her* mind. That is the first step in allowing her to visualize you as a possibility.

Guys who are permanently trapped in the Friendzone never get around to doing this. The woman that they are trying to get with never **visualizes** them as a romantic or sexual partner. Not surprisingly, the woman is completely **shocked** when she finds out that this guy, who's been acting like her best gay friend or her girlfriend, is actually sexually or romantically interested in her.

Many women are completely flabbergasted and stunned. Others **feign shock**. Some women are so used to treating these guys as mere friends that they are even offended. They feel betrayed. They feel used. They feel like the guy has been putting on an act all this time.
If you don't want all this drama to blow up in your face later on, you need to make your intent known early. It doesn't have to be a big production. You just need to get the idea out there.

You need to plant a **seed of possibility** in her mind. You want her to imagine the possibility of being in a sexual relationship with you. You can do this in a joking way, you can use a story, or you can tell her outright. Whatever you do, put it in her mind. Make sure that she knows it's possible and that you want that.

Guys who are in the Friendzone never do this. They think that just by being so nice and so agreeable, and by bending over backwards, that someway somehow she will develop sexual feelings for them.

I'm sorry, but sex and romance are not **door prizes** for nice people. You give tips to nice people. You don't get sexual with them.

<u>Why you need to flirt.</u>

You don't flirt and are not sexually aggressive or suggestive with your friends. If that is how you act around her, then you can't blame her for thinking that you are just a friend. You are not acting like somebody who is more than a friend.

Guys who are more than a friend will flirt. Guys who are more than just friends are sexually aggressive and suggestive. At the very least, they **touch**.

Of course you shouldn't touch that female you are trying to make your move on in an inappropriate way. But there has to be touch involved.

And, you have to use the word "date." When you go out, say *date*.

Flirting is a nebulous term – what does it mean exactly? How do you do it?

Cultivate strong eye contact, smile more, and break the touch barrier. Above all, don't treat her as you would treat any other female friend. At first, you might feel that you are crossing lines or being too forward, but soon you will realize that your perception of what is **forward** is probably wrong.

In fact, that might be why you ended up where you are.

One person's obvious is another person's subtle.

You might think that the signals you are sending out and your flirting are **obvious** to her.
Just because it seems so obvious to you doesn't mean that she can see what you are trying to do.

Different people process signs differently, and what might be incredibly bold to you might be little more than a hug to someone else. This is all to say that your intent might not actually be known – and you already know that making your intentions known is an integral step toward getting what you want.

Don't allow her to say *"He's just being friendly!"* when you take her out for drinks.

Be a little bit more sexually aggressive and suggestive. Touch her more often. Use the word "date." Constantly go back to this idea that you want to be something more than just a friend to her. Hold her hand. You don't always have to be verbal in showing your intention, and most physical shows are indisputable and hard to misinterpret.

Assume that she is attracted to you, and **treat** her as if she is sexually attracted to you. This is the final leap of faith you need to make. If you assume this and you believe it, it changes the way you act.

If your actions change and you are sending out the right signals, she will bounce back those signals to you. Or she will tell you that she is not interested. Either way, you get closure and can proceed from the Friendzone in a way that you never will if you don't take action.

6. When she says Maybe, it means No.

Maybe is a word that we throw around too often these days.

And you know what it mostly means? It doesn't mean that we're actually unsure and are considering a more definitive answer. It mostly means **No**.

We're hedging and waiting for something better to come along... which really means that we're not very interested in the person or thing. It's just good as a default or **backup**, and a way of avoiding having to say No right then.

So really, Maybe is just a way to postpone saying No. If we apply this truth to the women that we want, and to the Friendzone, it actually becomes a very powerful mechanism of **change** and for realizing what you've gotten yourself into.

Internalizing "maybe is a no" is how you can avoid entry into the Friendzone and the waiting game that inevitably ensues.

Like prisoners on death row, Friendzoned men keep hoping

against hope that this woman will finally wise up and see how great they are and become sexually attracted to them. They see themselves as **Maybes**.

As much as many women believe in romantic fairy tales and being swept off their feet, many men believe in equally bankrupt and unlikely romantic fairy tales of **overcoming** the Friendzone.

They pour their emotions and their lives into this woman. They put her on an emotional pedestal and treat her like a queen. She steps all over them and, at the end of the process, rides off into the sunset with a jerk in her arms. The guy's heart is broken and then he does the same thing all over again with the next woman. And she will treat him the same way.
And these men just don't learn because they don't understand that her Maybes are really just Nos.

<u>Don't be a Maybe.</u>

This law is annoyingly simple. If you ask someone out and their answer, in any fashion, isn't a resounding "yes"... **why bother**? That's all there is to it.

Why would you want to date someone who isn't excited about you? At the very least, that person should be as excited about you as you are about them. If you can tell from all the signals that they are sending out, from the words coming out of their mouth, from their body language and aura that you are a "maybe" to them, then it might be time for you to move on.

Yes, she may be hot. Yes, she's built like a brick house. Yes, she makes butterflies fly around your stomach. Yes, you see all sorts of amazing visions when you are with her. Yes, you think she is one in a billion (this is **false**, by the way).

But all that is worthless if this woman isn't sexually attracted to you.

Welcome to the Friendzone where 99% of the men in it feel just like you do. She's just a "maybe" about you, and hasn't shown any real sexual or relationship interest in you. Why are you going out of your way to pine for her and try to convince her otherwise?

You're more than that and you are better than that. There are plenty of women who would scream "YES!!!" to go out with you. Why should you need to **convince** someone to be with you?

If you cannot detect a "YES!" coming from her, she is not worth your time and emotional energy. Why would you want to date someone who isn't as excited about you as you are about them? It all really boils down to that.

Understanding that Maybe is a No prevents you from embarking on impossible missions.

If someone doesn't think Yes about you, why would you want to convince her to be with you? It is like trying to construct a huge building on a deep body of water. What is wrong with that picture? You need to build your building on bedrock. There has to be **solid ground**.

Does this mean that it is impossible to build on water? Absolutely not. But guess what? You are going to spend a lot of time, effort and money making it happen.

You are going to have to drain the water. You are going to have to lay down concrete foundations. You have to put precautions against water accumulating again. You have to do all that, just to build that building.

The same applies to building a relationship with somebody you don't detect as a definite Yes. You can't build a relationship with that person. It is going to take a lot of time and effort. At the end of the day, it is not guaranteed.

Why? Because they are likely to say Yes to **someone else** more readily than to you.

Hope springs eternal... but you should place your hope on something that gives you better odds and gives you the respect you deserve. Why would you want to have to convince somebody to be with you?

There are tons of attractive women out there, and many of them will say **Yes**! Focus on those women.

Avoid gray areas.

I hope I'm not painting a bleak picture and implying that you have no shot with women who don't answer with a resounding Yes when they meet you. But keep in mind that being in the gray area is not a pleasant place to be. You have to work twice as hard to get half as far with these women.

The problem is you deserve **more** than being in the gray area. You deserve more than pouring your emotional energy and your time - which is your most important asset in the world - into a woman who may not be there at the end of the road.

If you are in the gray area, you are playing the game to lose. Chemistry is a very big part of romantic and sexual relationships. At the very least, it must be something that you can detect, and that you can say more than "maybe" about.

The **sexual tension** has to be there. If you don't feel it at the first stage and at the first instance, then chances are not strong. Chances are you should just focus on her as a friend and focus on the person you can say Yes to (and who will say Yes back).

What I haven't mentioned yet in this chapter is the fact that Yes and the absence of Maybe work **both** ways. Just as a woman should say an enthusiastic Yes to you, **you** should also feel that same Yes about asking her out, about pursuing her, and about dating her.

If not... what's the real point? Just to use her as a **placeholder** until the next, better thing comes along? When you take a step back and phrase it like that, it becomes very clear that Friendzoned men have let themselves be tricked by constant Maybes when they aren't necessarily sure they even deserve a Yes.

"Maybe is a no" works both ways. She has to have a

package that is complete enough to make her worth your time, effort and energy.

Don't live your life through half-measures and maybes.

7. Establish yourself as a sexually available male.

As I have repeatedly mentioned, one of the reasons guys find themselves in the Friendzone is fear of rejection. They are afraid if they pour everything into obviously running after this special woman, she will reject them.

They are afraid of two things: (1) that they can't handle the emotionally crushing **sensation** of rejection, and (2) that they will lose the **friendship** they have with the woman.

They feel that if they are rejected on a romantic level, they are also rejected as a **complete** person.

I hope you can see what is wrong with that kind of thinking. You have to **compartmentalize**. You are not your failures. You are not your activities. You are not these small aspects and features that make up your complete person.

Unfortunately, guys who find themselves in the Friendzone time and time again do so out fear. They are afraid that being rejected in this one area will carry over into their self-value and self-worth in **all areas**.

As powerful as the fear of rejection is, there is another fear guys have that also lands them in the Friendzone. This fear involves getting comfortable with the idea of **physical and sexual escalation** – rejection on that level is truly a rejection of themselves as men.

These guys cannot handle physically escalating the sexual tension with the target of their affection. They feel that they have to treat women with **special gloves**, and hold them on a pedestal where they may not deserve to even touch them. They are, at the same time, nervous, shy, and wanting.

If you want that special girl to look at you as a romantic or sexual partner, you need to play the game of touching; break the touch barrier and establish yourself as someone that she wants to have sex with.

That's the bottom line of physical attraction, isn't it? One of two things happen to timid guys who don't touch their female friends: they either become **asexual** girlfriends to the women that they want, or are so unused to touch that they become borderline **creepy** when they do try to touch. End result: not someone that women want to have sex with.

Touch is the basis of **human attraction** and of those **butterfly** feelings in the stomach – what we call **chemistry**.

You cannot be timid or ambiguous. You cannot step back from the physical and sexual escalation that this relationship needs for it to go to the next level.

Gauge her reaction.

Think of yourself as a radio station. You start off by sending out small signals of sexual interest and then you keep increasing the intensity of the signals. The whole point is to get those signals to bounce back to you. This is a great way of gauging the sexual attraction or feelings of that woman.

If she starts sending those signals back, this is your cue to slowly take it up a notch. When you do **escalate** things, if you don't get a good response, if you don't get like signals in return, that's your clue that she is uncomfortable.

Does this mean that you are a bad person? Does this mean that there is something fundamentally wrong with you? Absolutely not. You took a shot and it didn't work, and you moved on. Actually, your ability to move away **increases the likelihood** that you will make the right shot and hit your target next time.

The point is that if you don't even take these shots, you won't be in the running at all.

Sexualizing guidelines:

1. Embrace the power of touch. This can be **subtle**, and should be subtle... but it should always be constant. Subtle ways include touching her shoulder or arm when you make a point in conversation, hugging her hello and goodbye, high-fiving her and briefly holding onto her fingers longer, and resting your legs in contact with hers when you sit next to each other.
2. Sticky eyes. Strong eye contact always helps, but what I mean by sticky eyes is to make your eyes

linger on hers whenever you make eye contact. This gives the feeling that there is a glue "sticking" your eyes together, and it makes her feel that you are giving her **special, suggestive looks**. This is a good thing.

3. Wandering eyes. Men that are scared of sexualizing hide their intentions. This means that they never let women know that they are looking at them... but they should occasionally. Don't disguise 100% of your wandering eyes on that woman, and let her know that you obviously find her physically attractive. You don't want to seem **predatory**; you want to seem as if you can't help noticing.

4. Subtle compliments. You can also use subtle compliments that aren't too forward or direct to let her know that you find her physically attractive. Complimenting women on their hair, smile, how good they look in that dress, or saying that they clean up extremely well all work. Shy away from complimenting them on their direct physical attributes like their body and curves.

These are elementary methods of demonstrating a sexual interest and of being seen sexually – once you get a feel for which of these you prefer and are most comfortable with, additional methods will come naturally.

Emotional intimacy.

Guys misread this all the time. They think that the only way to be intimate with a member of the opposite sex is through **sexual** intimacy.

While sexual intimacy is important and is one of the best ways to get intimate with a person, there are many levels to intimacy. When you get intimate with somebody, it can be as simple as her sharing a very traumatic story from her past that she doesn't share with anybody else. She doesn't only share it with her best friend. She also shares it with somebody she feels she can romantically connect to.

If she shares how she was hurt by past relationships, and that she is basically looking for something more from you – that is a moment of intimacy. You need to stop thinking that intimacy is just sex. You need to get comfortable with the fact that intimacy can also mean emotional authenticity and depth.

The key to avoid becoming another one of her girlfriends is to simply combine this emotional intimacy with a **sexually available component**. That combination is exactly what a mate is to her, and you need both aspects.

The touch barrier.

Go beyond how friends touch friends. This is very important. Look at how she is touching you. Look at how you are touching her. If you see that there is not much difference between how friends touch each other, you are not doing enough. You need to scale up your physical and sexual contact with her.

However, there is a warning that you need to pay attention to. Know when to stop touching. Do not creep her out. Guys who are considered creeps or scumbags don't know where to draw the line.

If a woman allows you to touch her shoulder, don't get too crazy and start touching the side of her breast. You need to know where the barriers are.

Escalating sexual contact and physical intimacy is an art form. It is all about reading her signals and about you sending out the right signals. If you get your wires crossed, or if you are clueless regarding the signals you are sending out, it is very easy to go over the line.

Touching guidelines:

1. As I mentioned above, the power of touch is immeasurable. It can take you from platonic to sexual status instantly. Review **Sexualizing Guidelines above** for a few easy ways to instigate touch.
2. Gauge her reaction carefully. You'll never get a clear green light from her, so take the lack of red lights and pulling away as a green light. In other words, in the absence of a No assume Yes.
3. Touching is more acceptable and innocent when there are more people around. You can grab her hand and lead her through a crowd, or put your arm around her waist in public – if you do this in private, it can be more forward and aggressive than she might be comfortable with. And it's certainly not subtle. So start the touching in public so you can transition more seamlessly to private.
4. If you attempt to touch, don't do it halfway. That just comes off as creepy and slightly perverted.
5. When you touch, come at her from the side, and not

face to face. Face to face is too aggressive and tends to make women uncomfortable. When you come at her from her side, you are able to actually touch more because the personal space that she wants to protect, directly in front of her, is still free.

Touch must be carefully **calibrated**, because instead of her feeling sexually attracted to you, she might actually get sick of you. Regardless of this risk, always focus on the fact that sexual attraction is the core of every romantic relationship. Make it clear to her in your own – but still obvious – way that you find her attractive.

8. You can't be everything to everyone.

This chapter will seem a big departure from the rest of this book's message, but believe me, the two ideas can and do **coexist**.

You can't be everything to everyone. What's your favorite food? **Not everyone** loves it, even though you might think it's the best thing in the world.

And just like food, you won't be **inherently attractive** to 100% of the women in the world, even though you objectively might be all that and a bag of chips. Avoiding the Friendzone is NOT just a matter of going through steps A, B, and C.

In some cases, the Friendzone exists because it *has* to exist. Why? The women you are interested in just aren't physically attracted to you, or they simply believe that they could never date you.

Hey, it happens.

You might think that this woman is the best thing since sliced bread, but when she looks at you, she doesn't really find anything worth being attracted to. Some guys are just physically unattractive to *some* women; some people just don't click. **You** similarly just don't want to date some women that are **objectively** attractive.

Does this mean that there is no way people can fall in love with you, or find something valuable in you? Absolutely not. Just as some people are drawn to Diet Coke, and others to Pepsi, people are driven and attracted to certain physical body configurations. Some people like baseball, some like football, and some enjoy golf.

No sexual chemistry or attraction.

Even if you look handsome to a lot of people, this is no guarantee that the person you are attracted to will find you equally attractive. It simply doesn't always work out that way; we all have our particular preferences.

But here has to be sexual chemistry, otherwise you are just going to be platonic friends.

Some of this is within your control. You can get in better in shape, groom yourself better, and overall work to make yourself more objectively attractive. But remember that people's tastes and opinions vary, so some of this is simply out of your control, even if you do all that you can to stay out of the Friendzone.

The role of other women.

If there isn't initial physical attraction, it doesn't necessarily mean that you are dead in the water.

In many cases, it might just be that the woman you are interested in has **tunnel vision**.

Maybe she has always been attracted to guys who look like Johnny Depp. But you look like Brad Pitt, so it's a tough transition in her mind. She has always defined handsome as Johnny Depp.

Now, if she has a girlfriend who thinks you are really handsome, and makes that clear to her, the scales might fall from her eyes. She might wake up to the fact that there are many definitions to the word hot, and Johnny Depp is just one version.

This is one way guys can work around the lack of initial sexual chemistry or attraction. Obviously, you need to be attractive to other women who are around the one you are interested in.

This is not always easy. In fact, most of the time, it is quite difficult. Still, if you are able to attract other women **around** the actual target of your affection, you might be able to get over the initial absence of sexual chemistry or attraction. It just signals to her that you have value, and are desired by other women – so why shouldn't she desire you as well?

Put in the work.

If you feel that you have been Friendzoned one too many times, maybe it is your appearance. As the old saying goes, "If you get kicked out of one bar, it is probably that **bartender's** fault. If you get kicked out of a hundred bars, it is probably **your** fault."

If you find yourself getting kicked into the Friendzone by many different women who look very different from each other, who come from very different places, and who come from different walks of life, it is probably you.

You need to take a long hard look at **yourself**. Do you actually **deserve** the women that you desire, and are you the **type of man** that they would desire?

Do you have the body of Seth Rogen? Then you need to hit the gym. Do you look like a young and broke Jim Carrey? Then you need to pay attention to your wardrobe, your fitness, your hygiene and styling.

The good news is that **physical attraction** can be worked on. If you are too thin, you can adopt a diet that can help you pack on more pounds. If you are too heavy, you can start hitting the gym more often so you can get rid of those pesky pounds. There are so many things you can do to work on your appearance. What is important is that you have to change your appearance the right way.

Many guys completely miss this. They think that looking right, as far as sexual attraction is concerned, is like going to a store and buying a product off the shelf.

If you want to change your appearance, you have to change your mindset. If you want to lose weight, guess what? You have to stop thinking like a fat person.

You start hitting the gym more. You start eating healthier. It all flows together. The same analysis applies to your wardrobe, your level of fitness, your hygiene and your styling.

Nobody is going to take care of you except you. Nobody is going to love you except yourself. Nobody is going to do that for you. So, take better care of yourself by adopting the right mindset.

The Friendzone isn't always the worst place to be. Sometimes, the greatest friendships you'll ever have come about exactly because you have established that there will be no future relationship or sexual tension between you two. Ever wonder why women love gay men? This is precisely why. They get all the benefits of hanging around men, being touched by men, and getting attention from men, but in a **safe and non-threatening** way that allows them to really open up.

9. Take a leap of faith to leap out of the Friendzone.

As I mentioned earlier, the problem with men who find themselves in the Friendzone is that they are **afraid**.

They are afraid that the woman who is the center of their affections will reject them and make a fool of them. They are afraid of showing her who they really are and what they are really interested in. It all stems from the same thing: the fear of rejection and the awkward and humiliating **consequences** thereafter.

Hey, I'm not going to fault you for fearing rejection. Who likes being made to feel like a fool?

But if you want to be successful in avoiding the Friendzone and becoming more than just friends with the woman you're interested in, you have to overcome your fear, get off the fence, and **take that shot**.

The classic strategy of being her **best friend** first so she will fall in love with you may work in the **movies**, but it doesn't work in real life. In many cases, you are just watering somebody else's garden.

You put in all the work to make her trust men again and somebody else swoops in and reaps the advantages of the work you've done.

Still, too many guys time after time do fall into this same pattern simply because it is the **path of least resistance** and it enables them not to put themselves out there.

It works exceedingly rarely, and it's probably not going to work in your situation. **You're not an exception, and neither is she.**

You have to lay it out there and make her know, in no uncertain terms, that you are interested in her. You want something more than just friendship.

She'll be oblivious if you let her.

You probably know the cliché about **assumptions**: when you assume, you make an ass out of you and me.

When you assume, you are thinking that what one person sees is exactly what you see.

Different people look at the world in different ways. We all come from different places and have had different experiences. Just because something is as bright as daylight to you does not automatically mean it's equally clear to somebody else.

If you assume that she knows you like her, and that you are demonstrating it to her in ways that she understands, **stop now.**

Women don't like to assume that about most of their male friends, and they also like to live in **willful obliviousness**. This makes sense for them, because most of their male friends would probably have sex with them given the chance, and living in that reality and assuming that truth would be tough to do on a daily basis.

So if you are subtly presenting yourself to her, **don't assume that she gets it**. If you let her, she will be oblivious to avoid a potentially awkward situation.

You have to be obvious and spell it out to her. Don't think that you only need to show her a few pieces of the puzzle and she will put it all together. You have to be a little more obvious than you think you are being. **And stop assuming**.

Take that leap.

I know that you want to avoid rejection like the plague.

But if you want to make progress, and you want a real relationship with that woman, you need to take that leap. You need to be **obvious** and say what you mean (and mean what you say) – remember that you can't assume that she'll pick up on your subtle hints, so being direct sometimes is the only way to do it.

The words that come from your mouth must indicate in very clear terms that you are interested in a relationship with her. This is how you take the leap. You do not take a leap of faith by being coy and dropping hints. The hints may be obvious to you, but they may not be to her.

The worst that will happen with your situation, if your leap does not succeed, is you'll feel **awkward**. That's the worst outcome, and not a life-altering alternative.

Now, what about the best case scenario of success? Lifelong dreams **fulfilled** and the love of your life securely within your arms? That's a **cost-benefit analysis** I could run with all day.

Be honest with yourself.

The problem with trying to be a woman's friend first and then trying to hop into bed with her later is that it is **fraudulent**.

The reality is that weren't interested in a friendship all along. You wanted to get into her pants, and the two became confused.

There's nothing wrong with admitting that because it's the truth. You may have developed feelings for her as a friend later, but the **genesis** of your relationship, and the continuing basis, is that you wanted to be in a romantic and sexual relationship with her. And you **still** do.

If that is the case, then whatever you have built is not a real friendship at all. It was something that was meant to lead to a romantic or sexual relationship.

Think about it. You don't treat her like your other friends, and you certainly don't have the same expectations. **So what friendship are you really risking when you take the**

leap out of the Friendzone?

High risk means high reward.

Just as when you invest in stocks, if you do not risk much you're not going to gain much. Think about it, if you want to get ahead in life, you have to get out there, lay it out there, and risk the possibility of loss.

This transfers to all areas of your life. What if you don't put your name into the hat for that big **job promotion**? Do you think you'll get it?

If you think this woman is worth the potential pain and embarrassment, you need to get out there and put your pride on the line. Chances are that it's a smaller leap than you thought it would be, and the **relief** you'll feel, no matter which way it goes, will be immense.

So is it a high risk? Arguable, but the reward is **literally priceless**, so there's no reason not to take a leap and tell her your intentions toward her.

10. Availability isn't always attractive.

Here's a little exercise.

Look at a guy who is obviously **infatuated** with a woman. Look at what good friends they are. Pay attention to his actions. Do you notice a pattern?

This guy makes himself available to her 24 hours, seven days a week, 365 days a year. This guy obviously bends over backwards to be available to her. This means that all she needs to do is pick up a phone, and he's there. It makes for a lousy game plan for somebody looking to get into bed with somebody.

Being always around and acting like her **personal sock puppet** isn't going to do you any favors. If anything, it's going to push you deeper and deeper into Friendzone territory. This is the last place you want your relationship to be if you want to get into her pants. It's just not what a relationship material man does for this woman.

You may think this is **counterintuitive**.

Women like to be taken care of, but if you take this to the

extreme and cater to their every whim, it's unattractive and, eventually, repulsive.

Very few women like to actually be treated like princesses and boss their men around – this flies in the face of what the majority of women instinctually want in a mate.

Time for some **introspection**. Have you been treating this object of your affections unlike anyone else, and are you bending over backwards for her? You're probably already in the Friendzone.

You know you're in the Friendzone when you find yourself being asked to pick up laundry. You know you're in the Friendzone if she constantly asks you to do her errands or grab a cup of coffee and bring it to her. You should have more self-respect than that.

Men think that the more time they spend around this woman, the more she will grow **dependent** on them. They are correct at some level in that the woman will find them **indispensable**, but for the wrong reasons and motivations.

The best course of action for you now would be to disengage and make yourself far more scarce and unavailable – in other words, more like a normal friend of hers.

Make it clear to her that you're not always available.

When women find that you have put them on a pedestal by always being available, what do you think happens?

You're **subsidizing** their behavior. If you noticed that she is pushing you around a little bit and asking you to do stuff that you really don't feel like doing (but you do it anyway out of obligation), it's going to get worse. If she detects that you're putting her on a pedestal, you're going to get more of the same type of behavior.

In fact, she may step it up a notch. Instead of becoming her lover in the future, you become her gay best friend. How is that for a **promotion**?

If you don't want any of that, don't make yourself **available** to her at all hours. Don't take her calls the moment she calls or respond to her text messages the minute it shows up on your phone. She's not above you, not a higher priority than your other friends, and doesn't reside on a pedestal for you to worship. Make it clear that you don't and won't give her special treatment, even if she begs and complains that you used to do it for her. This show of confidence and standing up for yourself can often have unintended positive benefits in her perception of you.

Men in the Friendzone believe that the more that they can be there for a woman, the more a woman will find them indispensable **emotionally and physically**. This is wrong for many reasons, but the end result is that you won't be viewed as someone that a woman desires. How often do you hear a woman fawn over someone that takes them to the airport, versus someone that they want but can't have?

Cultivating scarcity can feel artificial to you – after all, you want to do these things. The best way to back off a bit is to focus on other priorities ... and **not her**. When you become engaged in your own life, you become a far more interesting person. When you live for others, you make it difficult for people to care or see you as a whole, well rounded and engaging person.

Treat her like your other friends.

By being scarce and unavailable, you are actually setting up boundaries and healthy limits to your relationship.

You know that there's something uneven and imbalanced about your relationship when you drop everything just to help her. If you see yourself doing this, it should be obvious to you that you're not treating her like your other friends.

If it's obvious to you, it's going to be obvious to her as well.

As I've mentioned earlier, if she sees this pattern, you're going to find yourself waking up in the middle of the night because she needs something, and you need to run to the store and get it for her. You will start doing all these small favors at very inconvenient times because she needs it. The more you do, the more she wants, the more she expects, and the worse she gets. Now you're more like a **bike messenger** than a mate.

You know what the big difference is here?

When you cater to her whims, she takes you for granted and doesn't actually end up respecting you that much. She just doesn't if she's asking you to do all these things for her; especially if she's aware of what you're sacrificing to accommodate her. She knows she's taking advantage of you and she's enjoying the attention – all at your expense. That's not how someone who respects should treat you.

And that's another big part of **cultivating scarcity**. When you are not always available, ready to do her bidding, she will appreciate that your time and money is valuable and in limited supply.

<u>Treat her as if you're married.</u>

There's an old saying "If you want to kill your sex life, get married."

Basically, if you want to destroy the romance in your life, get married. There's no chase, no impressing anyone, and really no effort.

Well, if you want to throw cold water into the uneven pedestal-based relationship (friendship, really) that you have with the object of your affections, envision what your daily life with her would look like and act accordingly – in other words, like you're **not** trying to win her over anymore.

When you start treating her as if you are already in a relationship with her, things start falling into perspective for you. Just visualize it – you'll be doing all the **heavy lifting**, and she won't be reciprocating at all. The supposed relationship will begin to resemble more of a father-daughter dynamic, as you'll be taking care of her instead of the two of you taking care of each other.

And what do you get out of it? Let's say that in a long marriage, sex is extremely reduced. So do you get emotional support from her in return for your undying presence? Doubtful. Will she help you in your down times and carry you the way you've carried her?

It should become clear to her that you deserve respect – and a whole lot more – out of that relationship than you are currently getting.

Scarcity is the answer, but not in a way that you are playing **games** with her. Scarcity really just means that you shouldn't **focus** all your efforts and attention on a woman at the **expense** of every other area and relationship in your life.

11. Treating her like your girlfriend just welcomes the Friendzone.

If you find yourself in the Friendzone, you have no one to blame except **yourself**.

If you've find yourself deep in the Friendzone, the good news is that there's still something you can do about it. You don't have to be bitter, angry with yourself, resent or hate women, or feel that you're just unlucky with them.

You need to have a calm head and map out your escape. The most obvious is to treat the object of your affection just like any other friend.

<u>No bending over backwards for her.</u>

Stop making her your **priority**. You have to remember that she is not your girlfriend. She is not somebody who is sexually or romantically interested in you. You're obviously not her priority, why should you make her yours?

As long as you're clear that she is not your priority, two things can happen.

First, you can get your life back. Instead of thinking about her all the time like some sort of lovesick puppy, you can start moving on with the rest of your life. You're still friends with her. She's still in your life, but she's no longer the center of your world. This can finally free you up to find that person that will reciprocate your feelings.

Second, she can see who you really are. You have to remember that a woman can be blinded sometimes. When she sees that a guy is so in love with her and so willing to sacrifice himself for her, she starts to take him for granted. Instead of appreciating all that he's doing and all that he is, she just piles on the demands. She assumes that the guy will always be there to do her bidding. This is a completely unacceptable situation if you are the guy.

When you stop making her your priority, maybe she'll get a clue that she was treating you badly, or that she just treats you like a friend.

In some rare instances, she can see who you really are and what you mean to her. In some rare instances, she can start **running after *you*** for a change. Isn't that the ultimate dream of every nice guy?

Don't cater to her like a girlfriend.

You have to stop yourself if you feel your heart beating really fast after she sends you a text message. Ask yourself: What am I doing? Why am I acting like this? Realize that she is not your girlfriend.

She's definitely not treating you like a boyfriend. So get off whatever it is that you're on and look at the situation very calmly. Stop **catering** to her as if she's your girlfriend because she's not your girlfriend.

You may have all the obligations of a boyfriend to her, and you might pour out your heart, time, and effort to her, but you shouldn't expect anything back because she doesn't treat you like a boyfriend. It's like a relationship with **none of the benefits**. The only person benefiting is, obviously, her. Stop treating her like a girlfriend by making her the center of your world and dropping everything just because she called.

The pedestal sends the wrong signal.

When you put somebody on a pedestal, you're doing two things. **First**, you're sending a signal to that person. **Second**, you're sending a signal to yourself.

The signal that you're sending to her is that it's okay for her to step all over you. It's okay for her to take advantage of you. You have to realize that it's the worst form of **exploitation** when somebody calls at inconvenient times for small favors.

If you comply enough times, why would she ever stop asking? She won't. In fact, things are going to get worse. When you take her off that pedestal, you send a message that she's just like everybody else. If she needs something, she'll have to wait in line.

What's more important is the message you're sending to yourself. When you put somebody on a pedestal, you are training your mind to **worship** that person. You are training your body and yourself to make that person the priority of your life. This is well and good if that person is your child or your lover, but if you're not getting anything in return, you are just playing the fool.

Start seeing her flaws. The more you see her as a real person, warts and all, the easier it will be for you to stop putting her on a pedestal.

Above all, don't put her above all your other **priorities**. You have your own life to live. You need to move on and stop idolizing her. You will realize that all this time you've been reading a lot of your fantasies into this person. This person isn't all that, and isn't ideal. Unfortunately, if you are infatuated, you imagine this person to be something other than who they are. The only victim in that situation is you.

If you treat her like your girlfriend in the ways I've described, **congratulations**. She will never be your girlfriend because who wants to be in a relationship with a pushover, doormat, and people-pleaser?

12. Define your own value – outside of the Friendzone.

Guys who are in the Friendzone remind me of a story I recall hearing out in the wilderness.

There was a **monkey looking for nuts**. He found a tree with a hollowed out hole in the middle. He put his hand in the hole. His hand could barely fit into the hole, but with a lot of pushing and twisting he managed to get it in there. He felt around inside the hole and discovered the nuts. He grabbed hold of the nuts and you know the rest. Because he'd made a fist out of his hand to hang on to the nuts, he can't get his hand back out of the hole – it was too big.

All he needed to do was **let go** of the nuts so his hand could slip back out of the hole and he could walk away, survive and thrive.

The monkey sat there **helplessly stuck, but unwilling to drop the nuts**, and the villagers rushed out of their huts with machetes and knives.

The **lesson** of the story should be quite clear: **if you want to move on, you have to let go**. The monkey didn't get this lesson. Instead, the more he hung on, the more trapped he became, thereby sealing his fate.

Guys who are trapped in the Friendzone are like that monkey. They hang on to this vague **notion** and hope that the person they are pouring their time, effort, and emotional energy into will love them back. They don't let go, and never know when they should before things get worse and ultimately terrible.

This is why it's so important to remember that you have the option of **walking away**.

Just like the monkey, you can save your life, at least on an emotional level, by simply letting go and walking away. Never be afraid to **walk away or disengage** from a person that you feel you're in the Friendzone with.

When is a good time to walk away?

She calls you her brother, BFF, or gay best friend.

If she uses certain language that is highly familiar and highly intimate in terms of **friendship**, it might be a good time to walk away. We've been over this before.

If she refers to you in public as her brother or her best friend or jokingly her gay best friend, that should be a **red flag**.

It tells you that there is very little chance that she will develop romantic or sexual interest in you. You are safely segregated in the Friendzone in her mind. It's actually one of the subtle ways that she uses to let you know where you stand with her.

This should be your cue to start distancing yourself from her.

Does this mean that you should no longer be friends with her? No.

What it does mean is you should start taking better care of yourself emotionally by not hoping against hope that she will fall in love with you. Chances are if this is how she refers to you, that's probably **not** going to happen any time soon.

Don't let her frame the relationship.

When that special someone calls you a brother, her friend or her gay friend, it's too easy to laugh it off. It's too easy to just ignore it and not worry about it.

The problem is if you respond this way, you're just making the problem worse. You're giving the power in the relationship over to her.

Don't give her the power to frame the relationship. You need to step up and readjust it according to the terms **you** want. You have to tell her, "No, I'm not your BFF, your brother and I'm definitely not your gay friend."

You have to send her signals that you want something more from her. You want to be in a romantic relationship and yes, that involves sex. Be aware of how she wants to frame her friendship with you so you can let her know that you disagree. After that, the ball is in her court to make the next move, and you've done most of your part by readjusting the frame.

Always take control of the relationship.

Make sure that whatever it is that you have with her, whether you call it a friendship, a relationship, or a proto-romance, it plays out according to your terms. If you're playing a game, and you're playing based on somebody else's rules, the chances of you losing are quite high. This applies to basketball, football, and to the game of love.

If you constantly let her use language and frame your relationship in such a way that doesn't match your view of the relationship, you need to step up.

You need to make it clear to her that's not how you see your relationship. That's not how you define your relationship. If you don't step up, things will get worse, and you will find yourself deeper and deeper in the Friendzone.

She doesn't control how you are perceived.

This is probably the most important lesson of this chapter.

She's not in control of how she perceives you.

You are.

How? You are the one sending signals. If you have sent signals that led her to conclude that you are her brother, her BFF, or her gay best friend, whose fault is that? It's definitely not hers.

She's only reading the signs just as anyone would. It's you. You have obviously sent the wrong kind of message, said the wrong things, done the wrong things, or expressed yourself in an unclear way and that has led her to the wrong conclusion. The good news is if you can send signals to make her draw that conclusion, you can send a different set of signals that can make her reach a different conclusion.

Take time to work on yourself.

Don't be afraid to walk away if you feel that you're already in the Friendzone.

No need to make some sort of dramatic pronouncement. Just do a **unilateral withdrawal**. Spend more time in the gym. Read a few more books. Get a sales job maybe where you meet a lot of people and step out of your shell.

Take time to work on yourself. What I mean by that is that you need to work yourself physically, mentally, emotionally, and spiritually. Improve yourself.

What's the worst that can happen? The next time you see her, maybe your feelings for her will have changed. In the best-case scenario, she will see the changes and maybe like what she sees and start reciprocating the love that she wasn't giving you in the beginning.

So often we focus on finding ways to make the women in our lives want us, we ignore the fundamental question of whether we are inherently the kind of person that they want. So this focus on self-improvement and development can pay some very real **dividends** if you commit to it – and she will definitely take notice.

13. Women want your friendship on their terms.

There are a lot of similarities between the Friendzone and developing **cancer**.

When you develop cancer, it starts out with just a few cells, often undetectable. Those few cells get bigger and bigger, and they start spreading everywhere. In most cases of cancer, you only find out when you're past a certain point. You only find out when you need major surgery, or you've developed terminal cancer.

The good news is that with proper detection tools and the proper mindset, you can avoid going through the unnecessary drama, pain, and hassle of cancer and the Friendzone.

As long as you have the proper mindset going into a new friendship or relationship with a member of the opposite sex, you can avoid the Friendzone.

I've already gone to some lengths describing the warning signs and red flags you should be on the lookout for regarding the Friendzone. I've gone through several key things you should focus on when it comes to detecting the

Friendzone.

In this chapter, I'm going to focus on the **female perspective** a bit.

The female perspective toward their male friends, whether they are interested in them or not, is that they want friendship from them. Many women are fatigued by having to constantly ward off advances from their male friends and they just want to enjoy platonic friendships with these men.

That is, of course, their prerogative. They want something platonic and the men want something more than platonic but **neither party** is entitled to their preference.

Friendship is not a consolation prize.

You have to establish that you are not in the market for friendship with the women with whom you want a sexual relationship.

I know it's not politically correct, and it sounds crude. It may even sound rough, but if you don't want your heart stomped on and handed back to you all flat and bloody, you need to adopt this mindset. It's okay to be friends with women if you actually just want to be friends with them from the get-go.

However, you shouldn't look at friendship as a **consolation prize** after she has rejected you as a romantic or sexual partner.

Guys who find themselves in the Friendzone time and time

again are guys who will take whatever relationship they're offered as a consolation prize. They're thinking, "I get another chance at that prize," or "I get another try at biting the apple."

No, you don't.

All you're doing is settling for a consolation prize. The real prize, the one you wanted, never materialized so you swallowed your pride and decided to be her friend. What do you get in return? You actually get nothing, but she gets to treat you like a girlfriend.

This is a slap in the face to many guys. They're hoping against hope that this woman will eventually **change her mind**, see them for the knights in shining armor that they are, and fall in love with them. How realistic is that?

You might as well be filling out **lottery tickets** while you're thinking these thoughts.

Don't be afraid to say "no thank you" once she rejects you. You've got enough friends.

If anything, you're buying a **ticket to freedom**. You're making a sharp detour away from the Friendzone when you say no thanks.

This doesn't mean that your disengagement should be dramatic. You can just do it mentally. You can take the rejection with a nice big smile on your face and walk away. Consider this a declaration of independence.

The worst thing that you can do to yourself is continually engage in that pattern of being content to take second place and accept the "prize" of being her friend. You're just treating yourself like an emotional doormat when you do that. If they don't accept your affections, then in no way do you have to accept their platonic friendship.

<u>Women want to remain friends with you, even if they reject you.</u>

Most women are well-adjusted and are loving and sensitive people.

This is why many of them will want to remain **friends** with you, even if they've rejected you on a sexual or romantic level. They still see **value** in you. You shouldn't hold it against them that they want to be friends with you, after all it's kind of a compliment.

The problem is there is a minority of women who want their cake and eat it too. They don't want you as a source of sex and romance, but they do want you as a s**ecurity blanket or an emotional echo chamber**.

They want somebody, somewhere, somehow to take their call when they're feeling bad about Mr. Right. They want somebody, somewhere, somehow to come running the moment they call for emotional support and comfort. Obviously, this is unfair to you if you are looking at them as a source of romance and sexual attention. There is **exploitation** going on here.

On the other hand, great friendships have started out with

rejection. If all romantic notions evaporate in your mind as far as this girl is concerned, then it's okay to be completely friends with her. You never know; your friendship might actually be deep, meaningful, and grow over the years.

I'm not saying that it will grow into a romantic relationship. You definitely need to say good-bye to that idea, but it may grow into something more useful and meaningful as far as both of you are concerned.

Just because the relationship started off with a rejection doesn't mean that a friendship between you is worthless. What I am saying is that you need to stay away from women who use the Friendzone as an **exploitation zone**. These are women who really aren't friends with you. They are just using you, and they are not entitled to that.

14. Ladder theory revisited and solved.

I began this book with a discussion of the **ladder theory** of the Friendzone. To recap, according to this theory, once you find yourself on one particular ladder, it's almost impossible to jump from one ladder to the other.

You need to be fully aware of the ladder that you've put your foot on and make sure that is the one you want to go up. If it's not, you need to adjust accordingly – you need to step away from the wrong ladder and get on the right one.

If you want to be something more than just friends with her, you need to be on the relationship ladder. Pretty **straightforward**.

The problem with the ladder theory as I've mentioned earlier is that it is completely **wrong**. According to the theory, once you are on one ladder, you can't jump to the other one.
But you can.

You will have to work through many hurdles, and it will be a test of your character, but it you can do it.

In fact, if you find yourself on the ladder taking you into the Friendzone with a female you want to be more than friends with, make that jump to the other ladder right away. Consider it practice. You might not be successful with the first female, but every time you attempt that leap, you increase your likelihood of success with the next female in your life. Just as with basketball and football, the more you practice, the better you get. The same applies to jumping Friendzone ladders.

It's a skill you can **acquire**; it can be done.

It's something you can change.

If you find yourself constantly getting designated to the Friendzone, understand that this is **learned behavior** on your part.

It's a behavioral pattern that you fall into because you imagine there is a reward at the end. We're all creatures of the **pleasure and pain** principle. There is obviously something that you're getting out of this **unhealthy pattern** of trapping yourself in the Friendzone again and again.

This learned behavior can be unlearned – all you need to do is to focus on the **negative**.

If you always find yourself in the Friendzone, you need to really zero in on how much **pain** in your life is directly attributable to being there. There are no benefits to you – being able to avoid conflict and potential rejection is simply not enough.

Focus on the fact that you are living your life around **somebody else**. Focus on the fact that some of your friends are undoubtedly looking at you like a **fool**.

When you acknowledge the negative effects of Friendzone occupancy, you'll be able to stop yourself from stepping onto that ladder in the first place.

Be proud of yourself. You're a grown man and an independent person. Why should you sacrifice your life and emotional energy for somebody who is obviously not interested in you? Feel that pain, embarrassment, and shame, then use it to make you stronger and more determined.

This will help you see that whatever **emotional rewards** you think you're getting are not enough and it will increase your pain and outrage. You might be outraged enough to say "screw this" and make the leap toward the ladder you want to be on.

You just might realize that you've been conditioned to **complacently** fall into the Friendzone as a way to avo**id negative feelings**. This is not a healthy motive for doing anything.

You need distance and you must be willing to walk away for a while.

If you're thinking of jumping ladders, it's a good idea to completely **disengage** and take a break.

Distance yourself from the object of your affections and be

willing to take a long metaphorical walk. Think it through.

How does all this look to other people, and to you? What are you doing with your life? Are there any other, better options? How bad do you want her? How willing are you to sacrifice for her?

The biggest sacrifice is to risk everything and **make that jump**.

You're risking your friendship when you tell her "I'm interested in you sexually." You're risking whatever you've built over time when you come straight out and tell her that you want a romantic relationship with her.

So what's the worst that can happen? The worst thing that can happen is she will be out of your life.

My question to you is this: are you really *in* her life? If you cannot get what you're trying to get out of the relationship, are you really in her life at all?

Work on creating the best version of yourself.

Once you distance yourself emotionally from the person that has Friendzoned you, you should take stock of **who you are**.

List all the great things you have to **offer**. List the **dreams** you have for yourself. Imagine the **ideal version** of you. What would that ideal person look like?

Would that person have well-chiseled arms or a great set of

pecs? Would that person be thin, slim, toned, and good-looking? Would that person be eloquent and obviously educated and cultured? Would this person be funny and entertaining?

Write down your idea of the best version of yourself and **start working** toward that.

Instead of putting all that time, emotional energy, and resources into bending over backwards for the woman you're trying to impress, focus on working on the best version of yourself and then becoming the person that women instinctively want.

The problem with too many in the Friendzone is that they're so busy falling in love with somebody else that they neglect to love **themselves**.

Guys who truly love themselves would not allow themselves to be treated like emotional stepping stones. Guys who truly respect themselves don't allow themselves to be used up like emotional rags and thrown away. Love and respect yourself enough to work on the best version of yourself.

Take time away, become your best self, then come back sexually available and aggressive.

This is you crouching into an **athletic stance** and getting ready to leap across to the other ladder.

When you come back, be prepared to send different kinds of signals.

First, send her the signal that you are sexually available. **Second**, escalate contact with her so you come off as more sexually aggressive. If she rejects you, or she is obviously uncomfortable, then it's okay to walk away. What's important here is you walk away on your own terms after having made your intentions known. That way, you do not have to wonder forever what might have been if only she'd known what you really wanted.

By being sexually available and aggressive, I mean that your facial expressions, verbal signals, body language, and the words coming out of your mouth must all point in the direction of romantic and sexual intimacy.

Otherwise, you're just wasting your time and hitting the rewind button on the videotape of your life with her, and it will lead you right back into the Friendzone.

15. Other women break the Friendzone wide open.

If you were to do a statistical study of guys who have imprisoned themselves in the Friendzone, you would see a disturbing pattern emerge.

These guys are almost always **focused** on that one female, and treat her like the cure to cancer.

They don't date other girls; they don't even go out with other friends. They just wait by the phone or stay glued to their mobile phones **waiting** for the object of their affection to get in touch with them. They drop everything and rush off to help her or be with her the moment **she** needs something.

It is no surprise that these guys find themselves in the Friendzone. The more they engage in these behaviors, the deeper and deeper they get into the Friendzone. Eventually, they become the gay best friend of the target of their affections. In other words, they work hard, put in all this emotional energy, and at the end of the day walk away with a **booby prize**.

They all commit a very common error.

The common error is that they have **stopped** dating other girls. Other girls are no longer a possibility to them. They are putting all their hope on this one girl who they think will make them feel complete, loved, and emotionally validated.

You need to break this pattern and take the bull by the horns.

I've taught you how to detect the Friendzone and how to look for signals that indicate you're being herded into it. I've also coached you on how to conduct yourself in such a way that you can get out the Friendzone or from the friend ladder to the relationship ladder.

I've left the ultimate weapon for last.

This ultimate weapon is actually quite straightforward and simple. If you want to get over somebody, and you want to stop feeling like you are her emotional doormat, you only need to do one thing: **date other girls**.

This works on a simple principle called displacement.

When you are so focused on a problem, all your emotional energy and physical attention are directed at that problem. It eats you up and takes over your life. But, when you shift your focus to something else, the problem goes away.

When you start dating other girls, your presumed Ms. Right will simply **evaporate**. In fact, you might look back at the times when you waited on the phone ready to do small favors for her as a very funny (or embarrassing) time. Your

world veritably opens up, and your entire outlook is changed.

One of the first things you will realize is that she isn't particularly special; that the **idealized version** of her that you so badly wanted to be with was a figment of your **imagination**.

You can only get to this point when you start meeting and dating other girls. When you pine incessantly for that one "special" one, you don't even allow yourself to look at other women that way; you remain faithful and continue to build up that one woman in your mind. Doing that effectively closes you off from seeing what is **all around** you.

Maybe she isn't even that nice of a person, and it's just been a **habit** of yours to like her. Odder things have happened.

Talk to her about other women.

Don't think that this woman will see you differently if you start talking to her about other women. In fact, she's probably already talking to you about other **guys** she's interested in. Remember, she's treating you like her gay best friend.

Two things can happen.

First, she can actually help you increase your chances of romantic or sexual success with those other women with her feedback and input. That's a **win**.

Second, she may be thinking of you as her **possession** and when she sees that you're interested in other women, she might feel a little **threatened** or **jealous** and start looking at you as more of a romantic partner. That's another **win**.

The reason that we don't talk to the women we've been Friendzoned by about other women is because we don't want to ruin our chances with them by showing interest elsewhere. **Ironically**, showing interest elsewhere is precisely what will increase your chances with her because of the message it sends her. It says you are **romantic partner material** – if not to her, at least to many other women. And this is attractive.

As I'll discuss below, it just lets her know that she isn't your sole priority; you have **social proof** that other women find you attractive. All of this adds up to make her think about you in the way you want her to.

Show your value as a sexually attractive male.

The point of talking to that special woman in your life about *other* women is to establish your value as a sexually attractive male. At the very least, you're reminding her that you're **heterosexual**. You're not gay and not interested in other men. You're interested in women, and you're not a **harmless**, asexual teddy bear.

This is a very powerful reminder because you have to understand that when women feel pampered, it's easy for her to segregate you emotionally. You become some sort of emotional **eunuch** to her.

When you start talking to her about other women, your feelings and experiences with those other women, she begins to see your **value** as a sexually attractive male. If you play your cards right, she might even value you sexually. It's all about planting that **seed** in her mind.

Treat her like your other friends.

When you date other women and demonstrate to that special woman your value as a sexually attractive male, you also need to treat her the way you do your other friends.

Why? Isn't that going to come off as **manipulative**, and as if you are trying to play games with her?

Not if you talk to her just as you would with your other friends by sharing intimate stories and experiences. If you do that in a normal way, she won't detect any **gamesmanship**.

She will see you in a new light: as a sexually attractive male. And, she will feel a sting of regret or jealousy that you are now effectively neglecting her and have demoted her to normal friend.

People want what they can't have.

When you treat her like your other friends by talking about other girls, you establish two things:

First, you let her know in no uncertain terms that there are many other females out there worthy of your attention; she's not the only game in town. This might even make her worry that you've lost interest in her as anything other than a friend. Trust me on this: even if she had you squarely placed in the Friendzone, she **liked** knowing – **subconsciously or not** – that you wanted her.

Second, it establishes you as sexually attractive to other women.

If you put these two things together, it will make you more desirable in her eyes.

People want what they can't have. When you treat her like your other friends, you create a little bit of emotional distance.

Compare this with your bending over backwards for her. When you do that, you give her a signal that she can take you **for granted**. Why? She has you in her hand. She can dispose of you at anytime.

However, if you are this free-floating person who's independent and has many other options, you become more valuable to her. You become more attractive because she is no longer so **confident** she can have you or that you'll always be around. As a result, she's more willing to make the move that will take your friendship to the next level.

This leads to a **win-win** situation. You can break out of the Friendzone and realize that you can like and pursue other women. Even if there's no romance with the target of your affections, you already won because you have broken out of the Friendzone and freed yourself up to meet other women.

Conclusion

The Friendzone is where the hopes and dreams of many men go to die. And the worst part is that they aren't even aware that their hopes are dead.

It's not something that women do maliciously or intentionally to you. But it is something that they will do if you give them no choice!

Contained herein are principles that you can use with women and transfer to the rest of your life. After all, successful approaches to women that I preach – confidence, independence, supply and demand, and owning yourself – are really just life principles to abide by.

The life cycle of a Friendzoned man can be tragic. It's a classic bait and switch – only they do it to themselves. They imagine that what they are providing in emotional support and friendship will gain them romance, but they fail to understand the rest of the equation.

Relationships are built on emotional support, but they also need that spark of chemistry that is created by approaching someone **not** like a friend. If you think a hamster running on the wheel is a sad sight... But that's the old you, and I hope the value I've imparted in this book will lead you to exactly what you want.

Sincerely,

Patrick King
Dating and Social Skills Coach
www.PatrickKingConsulting.com

P.S. If you enjoyed this book, please don't be shy and drop me a line, leave a review, or both! I love reading feedback, and reviews are the lifeblood of Kindle books, so they are always welcome and greatly appreciated.

Other books by Patrick King include:

CHATTER: Small Talk, Charisma, and How to Talk to Anyone http://www.amazon.com/dp/B00J5HH2Y6

Cheat Sheet

1. A tale of two ladders.

Once a male and a female meet, a male will find himself on one of two ladders very quickly. One is a friendship ladder, while the other is the more desirable relationship ladder. How you conduct yourself will determine where you end up.

2. What causes the Friendzone?

There are many causes of the Friendzone, and they are mostly your fault for not taking action and making your intentions known. People don't like to be confrontational, so if you don't force their hands, they won't acknowledge your efforts.

3. Signs to recognize the Friendzone.

Women put you in the Friendzone in subtle ways, such as referring to you openly as her best friend or gay friend. These are intentional slips of the tongue as no one likes to constantly confront people on their affections.

4. Pedestals and the Friendzone.

If you treat the object of your affections like a queen and put her on a pedestal, you essentially give her no choice but to put you in the Friendzone. You just never feel like you would be her equal, so she believes it too.

5. Non-confrontation leads to the Friendzone.

Non-confrontation comes from both ends. She doesn't want to acknowledge your affections, but you also never want to make your affections known, even through subtle flirting. Action is paramount.

6. When she says Maybe, it means No.

The Friendzone is inhabited by men that are simply Maybes and backups for her. This should be insulting to you, as you deserve someone that can only say Yes to being with you. On the same note, you deserve someone that you can say Yes to as well.

7. Establish yourself as a sexually available male.

Women want to have sex with people on the other ladder, so you have to not act asexual around her, and make her sexually attracted to her. You can do this effectively through touch.

8. You can't be everything to everyone.

No matter how awesome the best version of yourself is, you won't attract everyone. You simply aren't some people's type, and that's fine and doesn't waste anyone's time. The Friendzone isn't always a death sentence.

9. Take a leap of faith to leap out of the Friendzone.

If you are in the Friendzone, chances are you are unsatisfied with the relationship dynamic. If you are unsatisfied, you should take action and simply risk rejection. There's a very favorable cost-benefit ratio for you, and you will be much happier with a measure of closure either way.

10. Availability isn't always attractive.

Bending over backwards for someone isn't attractive. It just lets people read so many negative traits about you – and they're usually right. You can combat this by trying to differentiate how you treat her differently from your normal friends.

11. Treating her like your girlfriend just welcomes the Friendzone.

Treating someone like a girlfriend means that you place extra priority and care on them, and this is the opposite of what to do.

12. Define your own value – outside of the Friendzone.

A relationship takes two to be defined and framed, so you cannot let her unilaterally place you in the Friendzone. Don't be afraid to walk away and disengage if you are not getting what you want – you are entitled to that.

13. Women want your friendship on their terms.

Just as you are entitled to walking away, women are entitled to wanting your friendship after they Friendzone you. But you don't have to take this, and that lethal combination can often lead to exploitation and manipulation.

14. Ladder theory revisited and solved.

The best solution to jumping ladders is to disengage, work on yourself, and become the type of man that that woman wants and idealizes. Too much time is spent on how to seduce others when it could be better spent improving yourself.

15. Other women break the Friendzone wide open.

While your time is spent idealizing one woman, you ignore the plethora of other options at your disposal. Ironically, taking advantage of those options makes you more attractive to the woman you desire because it fundamentally shows your value as a male.